LIFE COACHING QUESTIONS:

SUCCESS MODEL, GROWTH MINDSET, POWERFUL COACHING QUESTIONS, LEADERSHIP SKILLS

Table of Contents

Introduction

Everybody wants to be happy and prosperous. But how to achieve that? It's not something everybody knows. Are you looking for the answer, too? Are you one of those people who always strive to improve?

Here we bring you one simple and useful guide to encourage you, help and lead you on your way to the ultimate success. There you will find most effective methods and powerful techniques for self-development. We talk about the successful model, a great way to accomplish positive attitude and incorporate it into your life. You will find everything you need to know about the growth mindset - the fundamental basis which will enable your growing in every possible way. There are some handy questions which will help you in coaching yourself and get clarity.

In the end, you will find out how to develop your leadership skills, which are of primary importance for success in all the fields.

Thank you for buying this book, I hope it will answer all your questions.

Chapter 1: Success Model

Do you sometimes, or often, feel stuck and don't know what to do with your life? Should I break up, should I give up or do more, should I get my hair cut or take a rest? Wait for a moment. Take a sweet, deep breath. You need to take a break and think about your life. Where are you now and where do you want to be?

Have you heard about the success model? That is an approach which could help you move forward, solve some issues, or set and achieve your own goals. You can think about it as some frame for your self-growth journey. That approach implicates methods and techniques you need to learn and mindset you need to adapt to become the best version of yourself.

And there is one more good news – you don't have to look for a coach to teach you how to do this. You can do it all by yourself. At least, you are the best and only one expert when it's about your life. No one would help you better than you can do.

As the name says, this model of thinking and

acting will lead you to the success. You need to open your mind and follow all the steps. Following this approach, you will:

-set your attitude to the right, positive,

-sincerely see your reality, with all the good and the bad things around you and about yourself,

-set your goals – the big one, end goal, and more of the small goals which will lead you to the final one,

-make a plan of action,

-measure your progress,

-achieve the main goal.

How to think positive

Why it's so important? First, and the most obvious – it will make you feel good. Who doesn't want to feel that way? More there, it significantly raises the chances for success in any field.

Positive thinking is a skill, and as the other skills, it demands practice. So, you should do it regularly, on a daily basis, to experience the change. Here are some things you can include in your routine to become a positive thinker:

- Affirmations – these are positive quotes which can do miracles for our mind and whole life. That is because they are talking directly to our sub-consciousness. You should find affirmations that are right for you that affects you the best. These sentences are always in the present tense and first person.

- Beliefs - ask yourself, what you honestly believe about all the essential life questions – about yourself and other people, about the money and values, about love and emotions. If there are some negative beliefs, change them with positive ones. How to do that? Use the affirmations. Because beliefs are just things, we have heard enough times to start believing. So, you know what you should do.

- Do something that makes you feel good – this is thousand times proven recipe, and it always helps. Play music, go for a walk, talk with positive people or anything that makes you happy.

- Find motivation in true success stories – there's nothing more motivating than to see or hear about people who have succeeded in the same area as you want to. If someone could do that, you too can do it.

There are thousands of ways to help yourself to be more positive, and you should try as many of them as you need. The point is to find the best and fastest way to adopt a positive mindset.

Face to face with reality

Now it's time to think about the current situation. See your reality as objectively as possible. What's bothering you? What makes you happy? What do you want in your life, and what are those things, people, habits, anything, and you would like to leave behind? Are there some obstacles on your way to the goals? Talk honestly to yourself, and think about your personality. What are your strong sides and weaknesses?

Your current reality is where you are starting the journey of self-growth. Your abilities and qualities are your tools. So, you need clarity in knowing what it is. The most critical power which makes you strive for your achievements, like the fuel for a vehicle, it's the will. Do you have enough will to do on your goals? If the answer is yes, honestly yes from the bottom of your heart, the chances are you are going to reach your goals.

Set your goals

When you are sure where you want to get, it's much easier to find the way, right?
It doesn't matter what the kind of your wish is – is it to get your body in shape for the summer, take a degree or become a leader, the principle is the same and applicable to every field. Your wish can come true, but first, you need to change it to the goal.

You need to set your goals wisely. It should be big enough to be the achievement for you, to bring wanted changes to your life and makes you smile when you imagine reaching it. Also, you need smaller goals to show you if you are on the right path to the primary target and motivate you during the way.

What does it mean it should be wisely set?

The smart goals are much more likely to bring out the success. The goal needs to be specific – what you precisely want to achieve? For example, "I want to lose x pounds "is better than "I want to lose weight." It should be measurable and time-framed too. It's important to know how you will measure your progress. Our subjective feeling often is not a reliable measuring system. You need objective parameters for this purpose. For example, "finishing a project till May 27th" or "Lose ten pounds," the thing is that you will know for sure how your progress is going.

The correctly set goal should also be achievable and realistic. There's no point in setting some unreachable goal which would only discourage you and leave you at the start point.

Make an action plan

Now, when you have your goals set, let's do some crafting, and make a fantastic plan of action.

What should you do to reach the goal? What of that needs on a daily basis, what once in a week, how many times monthly?

To add some extra motivation, you can print the plan or draw it colorfully and cheerfully on paper if you like, and hang it on a visible place to remind you to stay on the way you decided.

The most important is to stick to that plan. No excuses. For every action, you are taking first, ask yourself – is this leading me the right way? Does this make me closer or further from my goals? Taking everyday small steps will surely bring you to the wanted destination.

No cheating! Measure your progress.

You have already decided how you will measure changes. Once in a few days, in a week or monthly, find some spare time to take a look at your progress. Measure it objectively, and be honest with yourself. Have you been an eager beaver or a couch potato? If you are not satisfied with how much you have done, don't be angry at yourself. It leads nowhere. Be kind to yourself instead, but commit yourself to improve your work on the achievements.

Celebrate!

Imagine how it would be when your wish turns to reality. How do you feel? How do you see life? Visualizing this can help you to motivate, but also to create the success. Creative visualization is the method many coaches suggest.

Once your dream turns to reality, it's time to celebrate, congratulate yourself and enjoy the success.

Chapter 2: Growth Mindset

Do you know the kind of mindset you have? For the beginning, answer the following questions to find out. Choose A, B or C – the answer which is right for you.

1. A person can be smart or dumb. The level of someone's intelligence is innate, and there is no much you can do about it.

A) Right   B) pretty much right   C) false

2. A talent is a gift. You can have it or not. If you are gifted, you can succeed, if you are not, you can try as hard as you want – it's not meant to be.

A) Right   B) pretty much right   C) false

3. Failure is an opportunity for learning.

A) False   B) it could be   C)true

4. It's essential to success. If you are not sure you can perform it well, don't give it a try.

A) Right   B) Maybe   C) false

5. You can improve your intelligence and skills if you make an effort, and have a good strategy.

A) False   B) Something you can, something not   C) true

If you have chosen A answers, your mindset is the fixed one. B answers say that you have a mix of fixed and growth mindset, and C answers manifest the opinions characteristic for the growth mindset.

Now, let's see what it means. According to Stanford psychologist Carol Dweck, there are two main kinds of mindset. People with the fixed mindset believe that everybody has a certain amount of intelligence, and don't see it can change. They are always focused on success, and they hardly fail no matter what happens. For them, a victory is a proof they are worth, smart enough, talented, and so on. They are afraid of failure and don't like to try new things. They are not willing to make an effort. If they can't merely and easily reach something, they would instead, give up than working harder.

On the contrary, some people know that the intelligence, talents, and skills can improve with a good strategy and some effort. That is the growth mindset. They know there's always space to grow and the brain, like the muscles, becomes stronger if you train it. Every problem is a chance to grow and to learn. When there are some obstacles on the way to the success, they make an extra effort or find better strategies.

People with this attitude are passionate about learning. They like to challenge themselves in new things, to grow in every possible way, and become their best version. That is the approach that makes a self-growth possible.

Both kinds of the mindset, fixed and growth, we learn and accept in the early childhood. It mostly depends on how did our parents and teachers treat us. If you talk to a child that it is smart, it will accept that as an objective fact and will not know to appreciate an effort. When it gets to some problem that seems hard, it will want to run away.

On the other hand, if you teach a child to right strategies for solving many kinds of challenges and working hard if it's needed, that child will accomplish the growth model.

Children with the growth mindset love to learn. They are

not afraid of the failure, so they are free to explore their abilities and improve them. Those children grow up among people who love to move their limits and who know they can reach anything they want with the right strategies and enough effort. This attitude brings them more success in every field – in school, in career, in personal relationships, self-growth, and emotional life. People with the growth mindset can achieve more, to become best versions of themselves and live happily.

So, if you didn't know you can change in many ways, that you can learn almost everything and achieve high goals, this is good news. You can! Your amount of intelligence, knowledge, talent, and skills are not limited. You can learn, you can practice, and it's worth the effort. "It is how it is" is the opinion which would make you stay where you are forever. If you always do the same things, you can't expect different results. If you are not cognizant of your ability to learn more and move boundaries, you will for sure stay on the same level of intelligence and happiness.

What you can do to change your mindset

1. Choose wisely

You are the one who controls and changes your thoughts. Every day you choose what to think and what to believe.

You decide how to think about challenges. Would you interpret it in fixed or in the growth mindset? Would you give up and run away, or make an extra effort? It's up to you.

2. Accept your imperfections

If you want to overcome weaknesses, you must acknowledge them.

3. View challenges as opportunities for learning and self-growth.

4. The brain is often changing, new synapses are making, and nothing is fixed forever. Your mind shouldn't be fixed either.

5. Accept the concept of learning from mistakes, instead of seeing them as a failure.

6. Stop chasing an approval. Focus on learning and growing your potentials, not the other's support

7. Enjoy the process. We grow during the process, and the final result is just the consequence. That's the price if you like.

8. Do something smart, don't just be smart. Reward an action, not a treat.

9. Talent without hard work won't make a masterpiece. The effort is that it causes change.

10. Appreciate feedback. Criticism can be constructive.

11. Afford regular training for your brain.

12.Commit to creating new goals to keep yourself stimulated and motivated.

Chapter 3: Powerful Coaching Questions

Coaching could be constructive not just in solving issues, but in avoiding problems, too. It can help you get clarity on what you want and become more intentional about your goals and actions.

Coaches don't provide answers in your name. They ask right questions. Right coaching questions are meant to help you find your answers.

Even without visiting a coach, you can use coaching questions in self-development purpose and enjoy benefits from them. By asking yourself these questions, you'll find clarity, prepare for action and discover new levels of your personality. It increases the possibility for learning and finds a fresh perspective.

For self-reflection, you will need some spare time alone to concentrate and dedicate to introspection. Writing is also a great idea because it gives you clarity and makes you slow down and think deeper. So, get a pen and a notebook.

There are some questions to lead you through the self-discovery process and help you think about the direction of your life. Choose some which seem appropriate to you and your current situation. Give yourself enough time to think about each question. It's the matter of quality here, not quantity, so no rush.

And be wise in choosing – pick the questions that challenge you. That's the way you grow. If it's easy, you already know that. Easy questions won't bring you profound insights.

Here they are, most potent coaching questions:

1. What is happening in your life now?

This question could be an excellent way to start. We need to see the situation as objectively as possible. The answer will show you where you are right now, not just with occasions, but with your attitude too.

2. What's missing in your life right now?

That's the missing part of the puzzle, with what you would complete the sentence "I would be pleased if only..." Almost everyone has their "only."

3. What would you like to have more in your life?

What would make you happy if you do it more often?
With whom would you like to spend more time?

4. What would you want to have less, or lose it?

You would be easy like Sunday morning if you get rid of that ballast, right?

5. What is working well?

There must be fields that work smoothly. It's important to mention them, too. You don't want to feel completely unsuccessful when it's not the case.

6. In what you are awesome?

It will motivate you and supply you with good vibrations to remember how great you are in some aspects of life. Be your best support.

7. What is most important to you?

So important that you would give your life to defend it. That's the central value for you.

8. Of what you are afraid?

What is your biggest fear and why? Is it because you don't feel strong enough to battle with it and win?

9. What is your biggest challenge?

That should be an essential thing or step you need to take which could change your life. It could be something you see is waiting for you, but you hesitate because of fear or don't know how to do that. What seems the hardest to do is the right and most important thing that you should do.

10. What are your biggest mistakes?

If you have already accomplished the growth mindset, then you should know there is no such thing as a mistake, only lessons. But you know what is that you should have done differently or shouldn't have done at all.

11. What have you learned from them?

Experience is the best teacher, so learn from the best.

12. What don't you want to ask yourself?

The answer will show you what is that you are trying to

avoid, but that's the crucial thing demanding your attention.

13. How does that serve you?

From this answer, you will see why you sabotage yourself.

14. If you could change only one thing right now, what would   it   be?
That achievement you should set as your first goal.

15. What does the success mean to you?

It's essential to define success and have the clear vision of what that means to you.

16. What would your reality look like if you were ultimately successful?

Close your eyes and visualize, imagine how you would feel, imagine taste and sounds and the smell of your success. How would your everyday reality look?

17. Why do you want that?

What would you be able, what would you have, and what would you feel then?

18. What keep you from getting where you want to go? Why don't you do that? Are that limits real, or you made them up?

19. What obstacles do you have?

Real or imagined, what is it that keeps you from reaching or getting what you want?

20. What resources can you use?

What do you have that you don't use? How can you benefit from that? What else you have or know or can, but didn't use yet?

21. What is the most natural step you could take right now to move forward?

It should be a small and practical step you can commit yourself to do for sure. Right now.

22. What would be your next goal after achieving the current one?

What else is meaningful to you? You should continuously set new goals to stay on the path of self-growth.

23. What impact would it have on you and others if nothing changes?

Negative motivation is still motivation, and it works, too. You should know not just what you want, but also what you don't want.

24. How will you know you have completed the action or reached the goal?

How will you measure your work, progress, and the achievement?

25. How will you celebrate the success?

With whom would you like to share your happiness? These people have a special place in your life. Visualize your celebration. You genuinely want that picture to become a reality, right?

26. What are the possibilities for the effort you see?

There are always many ways to get to where you want.

27. What options do you choose?

Why? What do you most like in that option?

28. What are the benefits and coasts of it?

You must be aware what you could expect. Every option has its good and bad sides, find them both.

29. How could you do it differently?

Think about the other ways. It's good to have it on the mind. Maybe some better way comes up while you are brainstorming.

30. Is there any more straightforward way to do it?

This question directs you to search for the most comfortable way to do the same thing.

31. How could you approach this using your strengths?

What are those strengths? In what are you naturally good?

32. What natural abilities do you have which might help?

This answer may guarantee you the success in natural abilities, and lead you to find how to use your gifts to get where you want.

33. When exactly are you going to start and finish every step?

Every goal, big or small, needs a time frame. Without that, it's still just a wish.

34. What would you do to eliminate internal and external obstacles?

Think about the distractors. Maybe you can eliminate some of them, and change some to the other form which will serve you.

35. What support do you need? From whom? Do you have it? How can you get it? Everybody needs someone to cheer them while trying hard.

36. How would you rate your commitment on a 1-to-10 scale? Do you have to take these required actions?

If there is some that guarantee, will you succeed or not? It could be the commitment.

37. What would you do to raise this level?

It must be closer to10 if you want what you say you want.

Chapter 4: Leadership Skills

Have you ever asked what those magical powers which make a good leader are? What do you need to be rounded by people who admire your ideas and like to follow you?

Being a leader is always a challenge. It means you have to make a path and set goals, make plans and be responsible not just for yourself, but for the others, too. As a leader, you have to evaluate when hiring someone, to recognize others qualities and weaknesses, to resolve conflicts and issues. It's up to you to give your employees and followers the example they would want to follow. Sometimes, it can be difficult, but it also could be a real pleasure and most rewarding position for one who knows how to do that right. Which traits and skills successful leader should have?

The key is in soft skills. Hard skills are specific knowledge and skills in one field, required for the job. On the other hand, soft skills are not so easy to define and describe - those are the personal traits and communication abilities, which are very useful for any job, also for private life. Most essential skills every leader should have are listed below. If you want to develop your leadership, consider improving those skills.

Communication

It is the number one skill which all humans need every day in every possible way. Personal interactions are crucial for good relations and positive atmosphere in the workplace. The leader needs to master all kinds of communications - verbal, nonverbal, and written. He knows how to listen actively, which could be not as easy as it seems; to be clear and concise when articulating and explaining.

Nonverbal communication is as much important as verbal, even more. The leader is great in reading body language and facial expressions, and he uses it wisely.
He is professional in other types of communication, too - in written correspondence, via e-mail or phone, in presentation and public speaking, in talking one-to-one or in front of the whole staff.

Motivation

It's the other crucial thing that you want to use as a

leader. He is an inspiration to co-workers and employees. What is the primary motivation to give your best? The money is often not enough. But if you have the sense of purpose on the work, if you know someone notices and appreciates the efforts you make, it could motivate. If the leader allows an employee the autonomy and provides challenging and productive tasks, the worker will be willing to spend long hours at work.

Delegating

Sharing tasks with others according to their abilities and treats is not the sign of weakness. It is a characteristic of good leadership. Pushing yourself to do everything alone will lead you nowhere. You can only end crushed, with too many tasks not finished. So, a good leader knows his employees, their strengths, and weaknesses, and he gives everyone obligations that they can handle.

Positivity

No one would feel motivated to go to work if there are dark faces waiting time to take out, to run away home. Positivity in the workplace is a must. Good leaders know that and do their best to make a positive environment. He is friendly, shows caring and empathy. He encourages and helps others. When all the employees grow these values, it creates a happy and healthy atmosphere where people love to work. Humor is also wanted spice, which every occasion turns into a delicious meal.

Trustworthiness

The employees trust only a leader they respect. A good leader knows that so he has integrity, he is open and honest and encourages this behavior in employees. He is accountable and consistent in response, so they are comfortable to step out with their problems and questions.

Creativity

Creativity is wantable in any job, but as a leader, you have to make numerous decisions which demand nonconventional thinking. Then creativity will create miracles and help you in solving many problems. If you don't always use conventional ways, you will inspire others. So, a good leader is open-minded, innovative, and imaginative.

Are you something or maybe everything listed above?

Some people believe that leaders are born, not made.
Others think that anybody can develop their leadership

skills like any other skill. We agree with the second opinion and think you can improve these qualities with right techniques.

How to do that?

1) Find your passion

People recognize those with a mission and enthusiasm and like to follow them. Find what gives you wind in the wings. Show others that you care, not only for finishing tasks but also for ensuring progress. It's easier to be all in when it's about something that inspires you.

2) Have a clear vision

Think about the final result you want. Set goals, main and smaller ones. Then, when you see the clear path, you can explain it to others. You should share your vision with the team, clarify why you have set precisely that goals, how you would get there, and how it would benefit them. Everybody needs a reason to engage in your vision.

3) Know your strengths and gifts and use them

Using your native talents and skills that you have already developed will help you a lot in becoming an incredible leader. Keep that in mind while seeking for a project that inspires you.

4) Live according to your moral compass and values

If you do something toward your ethical rules, it will make you feel bad. But not only that, it stays in your subconscious and makes you sabotage yourself.

5) Be a model, motivate and inspire others

When you live as you are talking, you become a role model and motivate others with your example. True leaders honestly live their ideals.

6) Master goal settings and following action plans

If you want to lead others, you first have to drive yourself correctly.

7) Have a positive attitude

Who wants to follow a grumpy leader? Nobody! People don't respect negativity. With a positive attitude, you will attract others and live a happier life. There are many ways to maintain positive thinking, so get to work.

8) Develop excellent communication skills

Do your best to improve your verbal and nonverbal communication. As a leader, you have to clearly explain your ideas, goals, intentions, to read facial expressions and body language. Active listening is as much critical as the way you talk, so pay attention to this too. Working with people, you will need to resolve some conflicts, and that's a particular skill, which you should develop, also.

9) Learn from failures and mistakes

Mistakes are a natural part of working, so don't let it discourage you. Use them as opportunities to learn and grow, instead.

10) Keep learning, educate, and improve yourself

Our possibilities for growth are almost limitless. Once you become a leader, set new goals and go on with self-development. The education shouldn't stop after formal schooling, which gives you just a basis to build your personality.

11) Ask for feedback

The feedback from your seniors and more experienced co-workers will show you if you are on the right path. It's beneficial to know when you make missteps, so don't get it wrong, be grateful instead.

12) Practice discipline

Everything you want to see in others, first find in yourself. Practice restraint and commitment to your work and self-growth. Carefully set goals and follow the action plans, measure progress and stick to your vision.

13) Learn to follow.

Real leaders recognize strengths of others and respect their visions and commitment. They are also great followers and willing to engage in other's ideas.

Now you have all the knowledge which you need to accelerate to the success. What you need is practice. So, start as soon as you can.

Self-development is a whole-life work. As every long journey, start it with a small step. Step by step, it will lead you to everything you want, the best version of yourself and dream life.

Think about your goals, in reversible order, from the end of your life to today. Set the big ones, and smaller. Make a plan of action and stick to it. Start without hesitating and follow steps from this guide.

Nothing can stop you now! Finally, there's nothing to keep you from achieving everything you ever wanted.